In the Footsteps of Explorers

Hernando Cortés

Spanish Invader of Mexico

John Zronik

 Crabtree Publishing Company

www.crabtreebooks.com

Crabtree Publishing Company

www.crabtreebooks.com

Coordinating editor: Ellen Rodger
Series editor: Carrie Gleason
Editors: Rachel Eagen, Adrianna Morganelli, L. Michelle Nielsen
Design and production coordinator: Rosie Gowsell
Cover design and production assistance: Samara Parent
Art direction: Rob MacGregor
Scanning technician: Arlene Arch-Wilson
Photo research: Allison Napier

Consultant: Stacy Hasselbacher, Museum Educator, The Mariners' Museum, Newport News, Virginia

Photo Credits: Werner Forman/Art Resource, NY: p. 14; Vanni/Art Resource, NY: p. 8; British Museum, London, UK/The Bridgeman Art Library: p. 27; Museo de America, Madrid, Spain, Giraudon/The Bridgeman Art Library: cover; Museo de America, Madrid, Spain, Index/The Bridgeman Art Library: pp. 10-11; Museo degli Argenti, Palazzo Pitti, Florence, Italy/The Bridgeman Art Library: p. 15 (top); Museo Nacional de Antropologia, Mexico City, Mexico, Jean-Pierre Courau/The Bridgeman Art Library: p. 16 (bottom); Museo Nacional de Antropologia, Mexico City, Mexico, Sean Sprague/Mexicolore/The Bridgeman Art Library: p. 15 (bottom); William Clements Library,

University of Michigan, USA/The Bridgeman Art Library: p. 20; Bettmann/Corbis; p. 23; Charles & Josette Lenars/Corbis: p. 31; The Granger Collection, New York: p. 5 (bottom); p. 7, p. 16 (top), p. 17, p. 21, p. 22, pp. 24-25; North Wind/North Wind Picture Archives: p. 9 (both), p. 19, p. 26, p. 29. Other images from Stock CD.

Illustrations: Lauren Fast: p. 6, p. 28; Dennis Gregory Teakle: p. 4

Cartography: Jim Chernishenko: title page, p. 18

Cover: In this fictional painting, Cortés meets the Native peoples of Mexico.

Title page: Originally from Spain, Hernando Cortés moved to Hispaniola and then to Cuba before exploring Mexico.

Sidebar icon: A stone figure on the remains of a temple in Mexico. The figure represents the feathered serpent god Quetzalcoatl, worshiped by many Native groups of Mexico. For the Aztec, Quetzalcoatl was an important creator god, who they believed would one day return to the people in human form. Some historians believe that the Aztec mistook Hernando Cortés for Quetzalcoatl when he arrived in their empire.

Library and Archives Canada Cataloguing in Publication

Zronik, John Paul, 1972-
    Hernando Cortés : Spanish invader of Mexico / John Zronik.

(In the footsteps of explorers)
Includes index.
ISBN-13: 978-0-7787-2434-6 (bound)
ISBN-10: 0-7787-2434-4 (bound)
ISBN-13: 978-0-7787-2470-4 (pbk.)
ISBN-10: 0-7787-2470-0 (pbk.)

    1. Cortés, Hernán, 1485-1547--Juvenile literature. 2. Conquerors--Mexico--Biography--Juvenile literature. 3. Explorers--Mexico--Biography--Juvenile literature. 4. Explorers--Spain--Biography--Juvenile literature. 5. Mexico--History--Conquest, 1519-1540--Juvenile literature. 6. Mexico--Discovery and exploration--Spanish--Juvenile literature. I. Title. II. Series.

F1230.C85Z76 2006   j972'.02092   C2006-902857-5

Library of Congress Cataloging-in-Publication Data

Zronik, John Paul, 1972-
    Hernando Cortés : Spanish invader of Mexico / written by John Zronik.
        p. cm. -- (In the footsteps of explorers)
    Includes index.
    ISBN-13: 978-0-7787-2434-6 (rlb)
    ISBN-10: 0-7787-2434-4 (rlb)
    ISBN-13: 978-0-7787-2470-4 (pbk)
    ISBN-10: 0-7787-2470-0 (pbk)

    1. Cortés, Hernán, 1485-1547--Juvenile literature. 2. Mexico--History--Conquest, 1519-1540--Juvenile literature. 3. Mexico--Discovery and exploration--Spanish--Juvenile literature. 4. Conquerors--Mexico--Biography--Juvenile literature. 5. Explorers--Mexico--Biography--Juvenile literature. 6. Explorers--Spain--Biography--Juvenile literature. I. Title. II. Series.
    F1230.C835Z76 2006
    972'.02092--dc22
    [B]   2006016036

Crabtree Publishing Company

www.crabtreebooks.com   1-800-387-7650

Copyright © **2007 CRABTREE PUBLISHING COMPANY.** All rights reserved. No part of this publication may be reproduced, stored in a retrieval system or be transmitted in any form or by any means, electronic, mechanical, photocopying, recording, or otherwise, without the prior written permission of Crabtree Publishing Company. In Canada: We acknowledge the financial support of the Government of Canada through the Book Publishing Industry Development Program (BPIDP) for our publishing activities.

Published in Canada
Crabtree Publishing
616 Welland Ave.
St. Catharines, ON
L2M 5V6

Published in the United States
Crabtree Publishing
PMB16A
350 Fifth Ave., Suite 3308
New York, NY 10118

Published in the United Kingdom
Crabtree Publishing
White Cross Mills
High Town, Lancaster
LA1 4XS

Published in Australia
Crabtree Publishing
386 Mt. Alexander Rd.
Ascot Vale (Melbourne)
VIC 3032

Contents

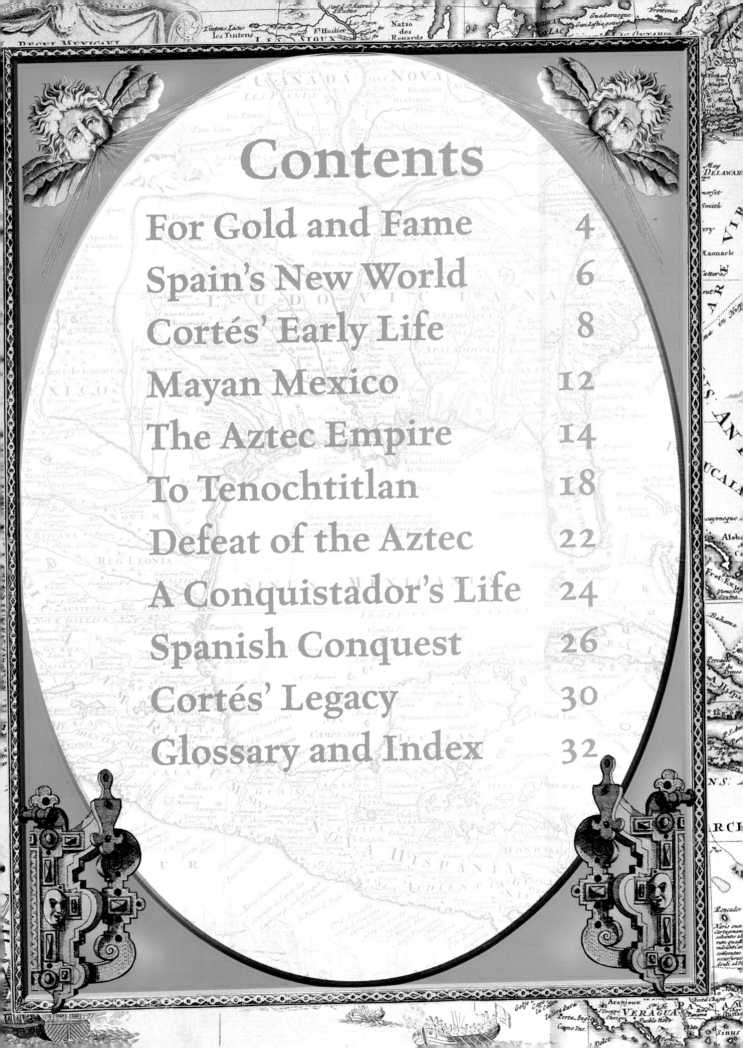

For Gold and Fame

Hernando Cortés was a Spanish **conquistador**, or conqueror. He led the Spanish conquest **over the Aztec people and their land.** Cortés' actions allowed Spain to establish a colony in Mexico called New Spain in 1522.

Spanish Discoveries

Before the 1500s, most Europeans did not know that North, Central, and South America existed. The areas where these continents should have been on European maps were shown as unknown, unexplored areas, if they were shown at all. Many Europeans believed it was possible to sail westward across the Atlantic Ocean from Europe to Asia. Beginning in the late 1400s, discoveries made by Spanish explorers helped Europeans gain a better understanding of the world's geography, including the existence of the Americas, or the "New World," as it was thought of by Europeans.

Conquistadors in Search of Riches

Like many Spanish explorers, Hernando Cortés went to the New World in search of wealth and fame. Early Spanish explorers conquered the people who lived there and set up colonies. Colonies are territories, or areas of land, governed by a distant country. Gold, food crops, and other trade goods were sent from New World colonies to Spain, making many Spaniards wealthy. Cortés sought wealth for himself, but he claimed all of his victories in the name of the king of Spain.

Cortés is remembered as a great figure in world history, but his actions led to much death, destruction, and human suffering.

His Own Words: Letter from Mexico

In the New World, Cortés went against the wishes of some Spanish authorities to take over the Aztec **empire**, the most powerful Native empire in Mexico at that time. Below is an excerpt of a letter written by Cortés to the king of Spain, describing his first meeting with Montezuma, the Aztec ruler. Cortés and his men had just crossed a bridge into the Aztec capital city when the meeting occurred.

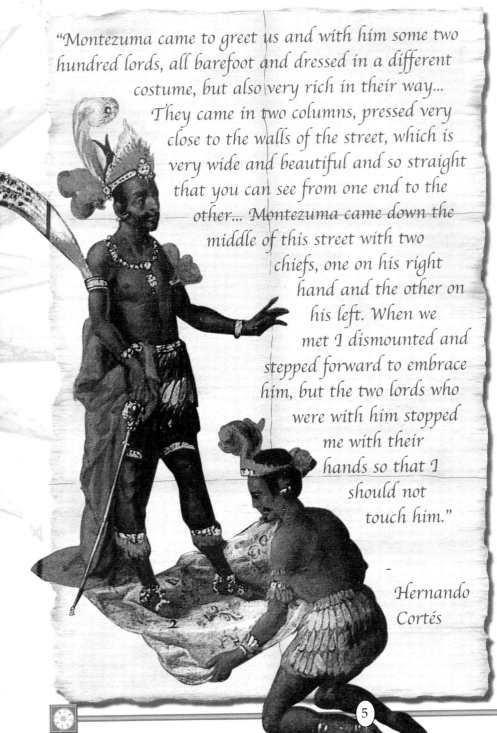

"Montezuma came to greet us and with him some two hundred lords, all barefoot and dressed in a different costume, but also very rich in their way... They came in two columns, pressed very close to the walls of the street, which is very wide and beautiful and so straight that you can see from one end to the other... Montezuma came down the middle of this street with two chiefs, one on his right hand and the other on his left. When we met I dismounted and stepped forward to embrace him, but the two lords who were with him stopped me with their hands so that I should not touch him."

- Hernando Cortés

- 1485 -

Hernando Cortés is born in Medellin, Spain.

- 1506 -

Cortés travels to Hispaniola, a Spanish colony in the New World.

- 1519 -

Cortés' expedition leaves from Cuba.

Spain's New World

Hernando Cortés grew up in a time when Spain's view of the world was changing. In 1492, eight years after Cortés was born, a voyage by an explorer named Christopher Columbus led to the European discovery of the New World, an area that included North, Central, and South America.

Columbus' Travels

Christopher Columbus was born in Italy, but sailed under the flag of the Spanish king and queen. Columbus traveled west across the Atlantic Ocean four times between 1492 and 1504, visiting the Caribbean Islands of the Bahamas, Hispaniola, and Cuba.

(below) Christopher Columbus was born in what is now Italy, but he sailed for Spain.

Spreading Influence

Following Columbus' journeys, Spain claimed islands in the Caribbean and began to settle them, conquering Native peoples who lived there. The Spanish conquest of the Caribbean began in Hispaniola, an island made up of the present-day countries of Haiti and the Dominican Republic. From Hispaniola, Spanish conquistador Juan Ponce de León led an expedition to Puerto Rico, which he claimed for Spain. Another conquistador, Diego Velásquez de Cuellar, led a mission to claim Cuba. At the root of Spanish exploration was a quest for gold. Gold made people wealthy. The Spanish created a system of land and slave distribution that rewarded explorers if they found gold. Colonies in the New World provided an opportunity for young men like Cortés to find riches and fame.

(top) Until his death in 1506, Columbus believed that he had landed in Asia, where valuable trade goods, such as spices, silk, and precious gems, were found.

Religion in the New World

In the New World, the Spanish met Native peoples who had different belief systems than them. At that time, the main religion in Europe was Christianity. The Roman Catholic Church was very powerful and had great influence over rulers and the daily lives of the people. The Spanish king wanted Native peoples living in Spain's New World colonies to be Christian.

Missionaries were sent with Spanish explorers to convert Native peoples to Christianity.

(background) Native peoples were often forced to accept Christianity. Missionaries and Spanish explorers believed they were saving Native peoples from hell and making a better world by spreading their religion.

Cortés' Early Life

Hernando Cortés was born in Medellin, Spain, in 1485. He was an only child, the son of Martin Cortés de Monroy and Catalina Pizarro Altamirano. Cortés' parents were part of a noble **family**, but were not rich.

Finding His Way

When Cortés was twelve years old, he was sent to live with his father's family in Salamanca, Spain, where historians believe he may have studied **Latin**, grammar, and law at the local university. After his time in Salamanca, Cortés is thought to have moved throughout Spain, looking for a path in life to follow. He saw many men travel to the New World, where they made a better life than they could in Spain. In 1506, Cortés sailed to Hispaniola, the Spanish colony founded by Christopher Columbus.

Cortés in Hispaniola

When Cortés arrived in Hispaniola, he went to see the **governor**, who granted him land to farm and Native peoples to work as slaves. The Spanish distributed land in their colonies using the *encomienda* system. Under the *encomienda* system, conquistadors were given land and the power to tax Native peoples who lived in certain territories under Spanish control. These taxes were paid in the form of labor or trade goods. Conquistadors were also expected to spread the Christian religion among Native peoples living in lands they were given power over.

(left) This statue of Cortés stands in his hometown of Medellin, Spain.

On to Cuba

Spanish **colonists** had been coming to Hispaniola for 12 years before Cortés arrived, staking their claim to land and enslaving the Native peoples there. European diseases had killed many of the Native peoples, called the Taino, who lived on the island. For these reasons, Cortés decided he would have a better chance of gaining wealth on other Caribbean islands. In 1511, Cortés took part in a Spanish attack on Cuba. The attack was led by Spanish conquistador Diego Velásquez de Cuellar. For his role as Velásquez's lieutenant, Cortés was rewarded with more land and slaves. Cortés set up a farm and is believed to have been the first person in Cuba to raise cattle. He also mined for gold on the island and grew wealthy.

(right) On Spanish encomiendas, Native peoples were forced into slavery.

(below) In Spain's colony in Cuba, the Spanish believed they would find gold and enslaved the Native peoples, the Taino, to pan the rivers.

Growing Excitement

In 1517, Francisco Hernandez de Cordoba led an expedition from Cuba to the Yucatan Peninsula, in present-day Mexico, where he met the Native Mayan people. Cordoba exchanged beads and cloth with the Maya, and was told of a nearby land with gold and other riches. Following Cordoba's expedition, Governor Velásquez ordered another expedition, led by Juan de Grijalva. Grijalva landed on Cozumel, Mexico's largest island, where he saw Mayan pyramids and other great buildings. Contact with a civilization that might possess gold caused excitement among the Spanish in Cuba, including Cortés. There was also reason for concern. Both Cordoba's and Grijalva's expeditions were attacked by the Maya before returning to Cuba.

Cortés Sets Sail

Cortés and Governor Velásquez planned another expedition to Mexico. As Cortés gathered soldiers and supplies for the voyage, Governor Velásquez began to worry that Cortés might be given more power by rulers in Spain if he made a great discovery. On the day Cortés set sail, Governor Velásquez hurried to the dock to try and stop Cortés from leaving. Cortés did not listen, and set sail even though the governor did not want him to.

- 1511 -

Conquistador Diego Velásquez leads the Spanish attack on Cuba and becomes the island's first Spanish governor.

- 1517 -

Francisco Hernandez de Cordoba lands on the Yucatan Peninsula, where he is wounded in a battle with the Maya.

- 1518 -

Juan de Grijalva, nephew of Governor Velásquez, makes a voyage to Cozumel, Mexico.

(background) Governor Velásquez provided Cortés with two or three ships for the expedition, and left Cortés to raise the rest of the money to pay for supplies. As well as using his own money, Cortés borrowed from his friends. He hired young soldiers willing to risk their lives for a chance at wealth and fame. Cortés gathered 500 men willing to serve under his command.

Mayan Mexico

In February 1519, Cortés' fleet of 20 ships traveled 120 miles (193 kilometers) from Cuba before stopping at Cozumel, where Cortés saw great stone pyramids and met with Mayan leaders.

Meeting the Maya

Cortés and his men preached Christianity to the Maya living on the island and were soon told of other white men with beards living in the area. Cortés sent messengers to meet the men, and discovered that they were two Spanish soldiers who had been shipwrecked earlier. One of the men, Gerónimo de Aguilar, joined Cortés' expedition as an **interpreter**. The other, Gonzalo de Guerrero, had married a Mayan noble woman and wanted to stay living among the Maya. Nine other men had been shipwrecked with Aguilar and Guerrero, but they were killed or kept as slaves by the Maya.

Native Encounters

When Cortés left Cozumel, he sailed around the Yucatan Peninsula, following the coast into the Gulf of Mexico. During Cortés' travels in these areas, he had friendly relations with some Mayan Native groups and fought with others. Most of the Native groups Cortés met offered him gifts of gold and food and then asked him to leave. Some of the Native leaders told Cortés of the great Aztec empire to the west, and its capital city of Tenochtitlan. Cortés learned that not all Native groups liked being ruled by the Aztec. Some thought Aztec leaders were cruel and did not listen to the concerns of the people.

An Early Battle

Cortés and his men fought the Maya who lived in a town called Potonchan, or Champoton, near the mouth of the Tabasco River. The Spanish insisted that the Maya give them food and gold, but the Maya refused and asked the Spanish to leave. When the Spanish would not go away, the Maya attacked. The Spanish easily defeated the Maya, and were offered gifts when the battle was over. Among these gifts were 20 Native women. One of these women, Malinali, became Cortés' mistress and interpreter. Malinali was also known as Malinche.

(background) Tulum was the largest coastal city of the Maya at the time of the Spanish exploration of Mexico. This city was walled on three sides for defense. The other side faced the ocean.

- 1511 -
Gerónimo de Aguilar, Gonzalo de Guerrero, and others are shipwrecked on the Maya coast.

- 1519 -

The Spanish battle a Mayan Native group, the Tabascans, at Champoton and are awarded gifts of Native women, including Malinali.

The Aztec Empire

When the Spanish arrived in what is today Mexico, the Aztec empire stretched from the Gulf of Mexico in the west to the Pacific Ocean in the east. From north to south, the Aztec empire included much of central present-day Mexico.

Montezuma's Concern

When news reached Montezuma that the Spanish were exploring the Gulf coast, the Aztec leader sent messengers to meet them at a town called Chalchicueyecan, near present-day Veracruz. The town was home to the Totonac, a Native group ruled by the Aztec. The Aztec messengers greeted Cortés and offered him gifts made of gold. At seeing the gold, Cortés became excited and told the messengers that he and his men "suffered from a disease of the heart which is only cured by gold."

Gold, Guns, and Horses

Cortés asked if the Aztec had more gold. The messengers said they did. During this meeting, Cortés showed the messengers his horses and demonstrated his guns and cannon to make the Aztec fear him. The Aztec had never seen such powerful weapons and were afraid. Cortés told the messengers he wanted to meet Montezuma. He was planning to conquer the Aztec empire.

(below) The Aztec ruled over other Native groups. In this illustration from a codex, or book, two Native leaders decide whether or not to join the Spanish and help take over the Aztec empire.

Forged by Conquest

The Aztec people settled their capital city, called Tenochtitlan, in the early 1300s. The city was built on an island in the middle of Lake Texcoco. A straight and long **causeway** connected the city to the mainland. Pyramids, stone temples, gardens, and markets lined the streets of Tenochtitlan. From Tenochtitlan, the Aztec expanded their empire by conquering other Native groups. The Aztec ruler kept control by placing nobles loyal to him throughout the empire. The nobles collected taxes and made sure order was maintained. When the Aztec ruler died, a new ruler was chosen from the dead ruler's family.

(right) Montezuma II became the Aztec ruler in 1503. He was the Aztec leader when the Spanish arrived in Mexico.

(below) The capital of the Aztec empire was Tenochtitlan, which was built on an island in Lake Texcoco.

Life in the Aztec Empire

The role each person played in Aztec society depended on their **class**. Slaves, **peasants**, and farmers were members of the lowest class. **Priests**, warriors, and nobles were higher up, and enjoyed the benefits of education and finer homes. Aztec rulers demanded tribute, or taxes, in the form of labor, and crops, or other trade goods, from the people they ruled. Some Native groups in the empire wanted more control over how their areas were governed. These groups believed they paid too much in tribute to Aztec leaders.

(right) Quetzal feathers were valuable trade goods among the Aztec. The long feathers come from the tail of a type of bird called a quetzal.

(above) Aztec musicians perform at a ceremony.

Aztec Religion

The Aztec believed in many gods and built temples for worship. They believed their gods lived above Earth, in 15 layers of heaven. The most powerful god, Huitzilpochtli, the Sun god, lived in the highest layer. Aztec priests performed ceremonies and were believed to be able to understand signs from the gods. Some priests advised Montezuma that Cortés was an Aztec god, Quetzalcoatl, returning to rule the land. Aztec legends said Quetzalcoatl would return to rule Mexico, coming from the east, in the same year that Cortés arrived. The Aztec believed Quetzalcoatl was light-skinned and bearded, just as Cortés was.

(background) Both the Maya and the Aztec practiced human sacrifice. At large temples devoted to the gods, thousands of people were killed as offerings. The Aztec believed sacrificing humans kept their gods strong. The Spanish viewed this practice as barbaric.

To Tenochtitlan

Cortés and his army established a settlement called Villa Rica de la Vera Cruz, near present-day Veracruz, Mexico. From the Veracruz settlement, Cortés planned to march inland to Tenochtitlan.

Forcing Loyalty

Some of Cortés' men did not want to march on the capital city. They were planning to steal a ship and sail back to Cuba. Some were loyal to Governor Velásquez, while others feared being killed by the Aztec. When Cortés discovered the plan, he ensured the men could not sail back. He stripped all of his ships of any useful items, including sails, oars, and metal parts, and then destroyed most of his fleet.

March to the Capital

Cortés left 100 of his men behind to guard the Veracruz settlement. The rest began the more than 400-mile (644-kilometer) overland march to Tenochtitlan. Cortés and his men traveled through Aztec towns, where they met local leaders and preached the Christian religion. While some Native communities welcomed the Spanish, others did not.

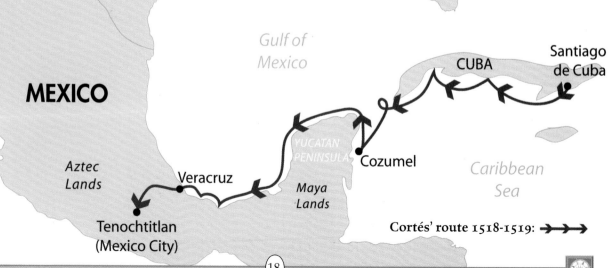

MEXICO

Gulf of Mexico

CUBA

Santiago de Cuba

YUCATÁN PENINSULA

Cozumel

Caribbean Sea

Aztec Lands

Veracruz

Maya Lands

Tenochtitlan (Mexico City)

Cortés' route 1518-1519: ➤➤➤

The Tlaxcalans

On their way to Tenochtitlan, the Spanish traveled through an area called Tlaxcala. The Tlaxcalan people were enemies of the Aztec and their land was not part of the Aztec empire. Unsure if the Spanish planned to destroy them, the Tlaxcalans fought against Cortés' army. After a two-week conflict, the Tlaxcalans gave in and formed an **alliance** with Cortés to fight the Aztec. The Spanish and Tlaxcalans marched together to Tenochtitlan.

(background) Cortés claimed that 150,000 Tlaxcalans fought his few hundred Spanish soldiers. Even though the Spanish were outnumbered, European-made weapons helped ensure a victory.

- August 16, 1519 -

Cortés' expedition leaves the Veracruz settlement. Marching with the Spanish soldiers are warriors and allies from the Totonac Native group.

- September 1519 -

The Spanish battle with the Tlaxcalans.

- October 23, 1519 -

Cortés once again sets out for Tenochtitlan, this time with a larger army, including Tlaxcalan warriors.

Ruthless Killing

On the way to Tenochtitlan, the Tlaxcalans and Spaniards stopped in Cholula. The Tlaxcalans told Cortés that the Cholulans were planning to trap and kill him. Cortés ordered his army to attack the Cholulans. When word of the attack spread, Native peoples who lived in nearby Aztec towns became fearful. Cortés believed that if he could make the Aztec fear him, they would be easier to defeat. After leaving Cholula, Cortés traveled to villages surrounding Tenochtitlan to gain support for his attack on the Aztec capital city. Most Native peoples were afraid of what Cortés might do if they did not join.

Into the City

When Cortés, his Spanish soldiers, and Native allies marched into Tenochtitlan, the people who lived in the city lined the causeway and streets to see them arrive. Montezuma treated Cortés as a guest, offering him gifts and giving him a tour of the city. The Aztec leader was still not sure what Cortés was planning, but found out eight days later when Cortés took Montezuma prisoner. Cortés told Montezuma to continue ruling his empire as if all was normal.

(above) After launching an unprovoked attack, Cortés' army slaughtered 3,000 Cholulans.

Divided Force

Montezuma was still Cortés' prisoner when Cortés learned that a large group of Spanish soldiers had landed at the Veracruz settlement. The force had been sent by Governor Velásquez to stop Cortés. Cortés took 120 men to meet the Spanish army and left Tenochtitlan under the command of conquistador Pedro de Alvarado. During the night, Cortés launched an attack on the Spanish force at Veracruz. Cortés and his men won the battle. When the fighting was over, Cortés convinced Spanish soldiers sent by the governor to join him in fighting the Aztec. Cortés promised the soldiers gold and riches would come with victory at Tenochtitlan.

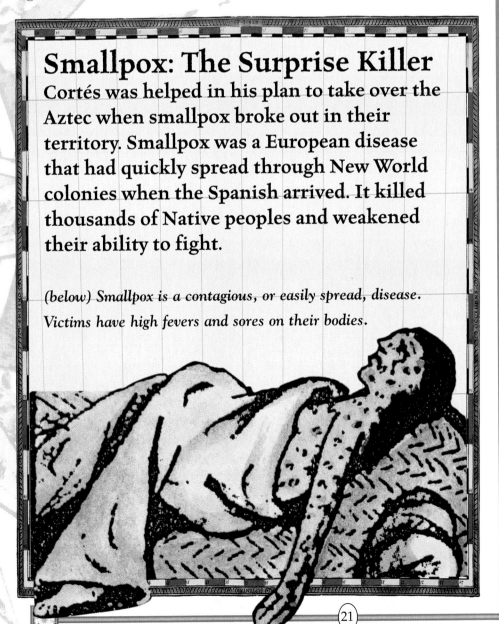

Smallpox: The Surprise Killer

Cortés was helped in his plan to take over the Aztec when smallpox broke out in their territory. Smallpox was a European disease that had quickly spread through New World colonies when the Spanish arrived. It killed thousands of Native peoples and weakened their ability to fight.

(below) Smallpox is a contagious, or easily spread, disease. Victims have high fevers and sores on their bodies.

- November 8, 1519 -

Cortés and his Native allies arrive in Tenochtitlan.

- November 16, 1519 -

Cortés makes Montezuma his prisoner.

- April 1520 -

Cortés learns of Spanish landing at Veracruz.

Defeat of the Aztec

While Cortés was meeting the Spanish at Veracruz, Alvarado imprisoned and killed some Aztec leaders, and Spanish soldiers attacked and killed city residents at an Aztec spring festival. In return, the Aztec began to organize to fight the Spanish.

Spanish Escape

When Cortés arrived back in Tenochtitlan, the Aztec cut off the causeway leading out of the city and began to starve the Spanish of food and water. Cortés planned to escape from the city during the night. When the Aztec saw the Spanish fleeing, fighting broke out. More than 600 of Cortés' soldiers were killed, but their leader escaped. Cortés led his surviving soldiers back to Tlaxcala, where he began to prepare for another attack.

Final Battle

Cortés planned to attack Tenochtitlan using boats because the Aztec had cut off the city's causeway. Eight thousand Native peoples carried parts of boats from Tlaxcala to the lake surrounding Tenochtitlan, then built and launched them. Cortés and his men landed in Tenochtitlan and began fighting their way through the streets. Thousands of Aztec and other Native peoples were killed in the battle. The final battle for Tenochtitlan lasted 80 days. During this time, the Spanish cut off the Aztec's supply of food and water. Some accounts say that a total of 100,000 Native peoples were killed during fighting. The Aztec surrender of Tenochtitlan came on August 13, 1521. Cortés wrote a letter to the king of Spain to report his victory, and was rewarded with royal permission to rule over the conquered territory.

(left) At an Aztec spring festival, unarmed dancers, singers, and spectators were massacred by Spanish soldiers, as ordered by Pedro de Alvarado.

(background) Cortés sent Montezuma out to talk to the people in an effort to help the Spanish. While Montezuma talked from a balcony, the Aztec who had gathered began to throw things at him. Spanish accounts say Montezuma was hit by a rock and later died from his injury. Montezuma's death angered the Aztec, who blamed the Spanish for killing him.

A Conquistador's Life

Conquistadors were Spanish explorers and soldiers who traveled to the New World to try to gain wealth and positions of power. Conquistadors craved fame, adventure, and gold. After discovering new lands, conquistadors could be granted permission from the Spanish king to rule them.

Weapons of War

As well as weapons made of metal, Cortés' army used horses to help win battles against Native forces. The Aztec had never before seen horses, and many were frightened by them. Some Native peoples mistook the horses for a kind of deer or for dragons. Others thought Spanish soldiers riding on their horses were four-legged animals with human upper bodies. Spanish armor, metal swords and lances, and guns also **intimidated** the Aztec, who had never encountered such weapons of war.

(background) About 500 sailors and soldiers were under Cortés' command when his fleet of 20 ships left Cuba. Cortés' ships were stocked with guns, cannon, and other weapons, as well as the materials needed to build a new Spanish settlement.

Gifts of Women

During their travels, conquistadors were offered women as gifts by Native groups. These women were usually captives from battles between Native groups, or had been sold into slavery by their families. The Spanish used the women as slaves, to cook food and care for them. Native women were also kept as the mistresses of conquistadors. Relationships between Spanish men and Native women led to the birth of the first people with mixed Spanish and Native **ancestry**. Most modern-day Mexicans claim mixed Spanish and Native ancestry.

(below) Malinali was Cortés' interpreter and mistress. She later gave birth to Cortés' son.

Aztec Hot Chocolate

A favorite Aztec drink was *chocolatl*, which was made from cacao beans. The Aztec added chilies and other spices to *chocolatl*. Ask an adult to help you prepare this modern version of *chocolatl*.

Ingredients:

2 cups (478 mL) boiling water
1 chili pepper, cut in half, seeds removed
5 cups (1.2 L) light cream
1 cinnamon stick
8 ounces (227 g) bittersweet chocolate
2 tablespoons (30 mL) honey
1 tablespoon (15 mL) ground almonds or hazelnuts

Directions:

1. Bring water to boil over medium-high heat. Add chili pepper.
2. Boil down until liquid is half evaporated, and remove chili pepper using a strainer. Set water aside.
3. In another pan, warm cream and cinnamon stick over medium heat until bubbles appear around the edge.
4. Reduce heat to low and add chocolate and honey. Stir until chocolate is melted, then remove cinnamon stick.
5. Add water from boiled chili a little at a time to taste. Add milk if the drink is too thick.
6. Top with ground almonds or hazelnuts.

Spanish Conquest

The Spanish conquest of Mexico was not a single event, but continued after the fall of Tenochtitlan. The Conquest of Mexico is the name given to the period when the Spanish began conquering and settling Aztec lands, leading to the creation of New Spain.

Ruined Capital

After the fall of Tenochtitlan, Spanish forces were left to rule over a ruined city. The bodies of Native soldiers littered the streets and Aztec buildings were destroyed. Aztec soldiers who survived the battle were forced to work as slaves. These slaves worked rebuilding the city, and in Spanish gold and silver mines. Catholic churches were built on top of ruined Aztec temples and European-style buildings replaced traditional structures. Catholic priests worked to convert the Aztec to Christianity, while conquistadors were sent to take over surrounding areas.

(background) Cortés had Native slaves build a house for him in Tenochtitlan, which was renamed Mexico City.

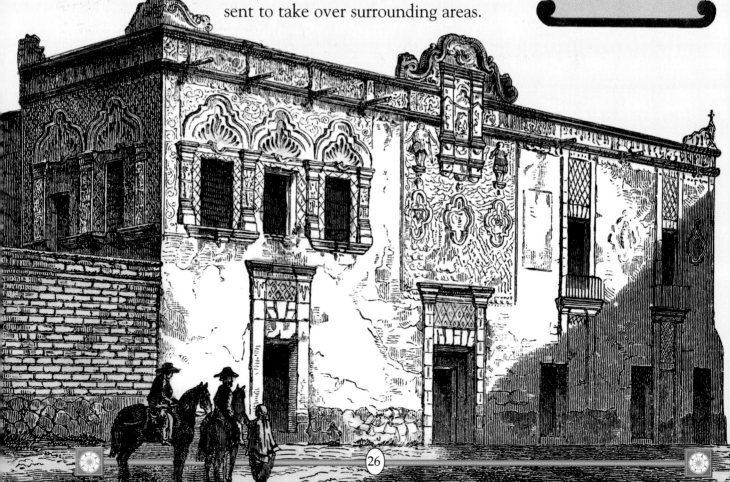

(above) Some Spanish colonists were cruel to the Native peoples of Mexico. Native peoples were forced into labor in mines and on farms and were denied the right to practice their own religion.

Seeking Gold

Cortés had little gold or silver to share with his men following the siege of Tenochtitlan. So little gold had been found that the Spanish believed the Aztec had removed golden objects from the city so they would not be stolen. Most of the Aztec artifacts the Spanish did find were melted down and sent back to Spain. Instead of rewarding his soldiers with gold, Cortés gave them land on which to farm and Native slaves to work the land. The Spanish continued their search for gold after the fall of Tenochtitlan, even executing some Aztec leaders who refused to say where the Spanish might find gold. The Aztec people, weakened by European diseases that spread throughout New Spain, could not mount a strong opposition to fight the Spanish.

(above) Francisco Pizarro was a Spanish conquistador. Beginning in 1531, he led the Spanish attack on the Inca people in Peru, in South America. Pizarro, who dreamed of becoming rich through conquest, was inspired by Cortés' defeat of the Aztec.

Changing Lives

Thousands of Spanish colonists flooded into New Spain. The newcomers included merchants, tradespeople, and church leaders. The Spanish took over Aztec lands and banned Aztec religious ceremonies. Despite these actions, some Aztec eventually adopted aspects of Christianity and the European way of life. Some Native peoples who converted to Christianity were allowed to keep their wealth. Cortés worked to ensure Spanish control over what had been the Aztec empire. In governing, Cortés kept traditional leaders in place and demanded tribute, or taxes, in goods or labor. When a conquistador was given Native peoples as slave workers, Cortés ordered that the slaves be treated well. Despite this, many slaves were treated badly by their Spanish rulers.

The End of Cortés

Cortés returned to Spain a hero in 1528, the year he met with the king. Even though he had become wealthy, Cortés was not ready to settle in Europe. He returned to Mexico in 1530, still hoping to find gold. Cortés was unsuccessful in finding any great amount of gold and returned to Spain ten years later a less popular man than when he had led the attack on the Aztec empire. He moved to Seville, Spain, where he later died at the age of 62. Cortés' letters that he had sent to the Spanish king describing his adventures and accomplishments were published and became a popular book in Spain.

(background) Cortés received a hero's welcome when he returned to Spain to meet with King Carlos I, who was also known as Charles V.

- 1528 -

Cortés returns to Spain a hero.

- 1530 -

Cortés travels to Mexico seeking gold.

- 1540 -

Cortés makes his final return to Spain.

- December 2, 1547 -

Cortés dies near Seville, Spain.

Cortés' Legacy

Hernando Cortés is an important figure in world history, but not a well-liked figure in present-day Mexico. He is remembered as the person responsible for the destruction of Aztec culture and way of life.

Vanishing Culture

In the years following the Aztec surrender at Tenochtitlan, the Spanish came to control all of what would become Mexico. Many Aztec and Maya died when Europeans brought new diseases, including smallpox, measles, and mumps. Despite the downfall of Native culture, some Aztec and Maya ruins have survived and can still be seen today. Some Aztec artifacts sent to Europe in the time of Cortés also still exist. Many modern-day Mexicans have Aztec and Mayan ancestors. Over the years, many Spanish and Native peoples married, creating families of mixed European and Native backgrounds.

Many plants that are familiar around the world today were first grown in the New World. This includes corn, tomatoes, and chili peppers. Spanish explorers introduced these foods to Europe.

Changing Europe

Spain and all of Europe benefited from Cortés' discoveries, which led to increased wealth through the trade of gold, silver, tobacco, cacao beans, and other items. Cortés also helped further develop European understanding of New World geography. After the fall of Tenochtitlan, Spanish conquistadors reached the Pacific coast of Mexico. Following Cortés, mapmakers charted the coast of Mexico and other areas nearby. Eventually, European sailors knew that a large body of land, which included North and South America, lay between Europe and Asia.

Probanzas and the Spanish Conquest

The role of the conquistadors in the Spanish conquest of Central and South America is debated by historians today. The main sources of information about the conquest are firsthand reports written by the conquistadors and their men, which were sent back to the Spanish king. These reports, called probanzas, were written to prove to the king that the conqueror deserved rewards, such as titles and pensions, for their work. Some historians today question the facts presented by the conquistadors in these reports, and the role that individuals played in the conquest. The information on events and people in this book are based on the probanzas and some historians' interpretations of these reports.

Artwork

There were no cameras or video recording equipment during the Spanish conquest. Much of the artwork in this book was created later by artists who were not present at the events. For this reason, the events may not have happened exactly as they appear in this book, but in styles that were popular during an artist's lifetime.

(right) This image shows part of a painting by Mexican artist Diego Rivera. It is called The Great Tenochtitlan. *The Aztec city was destroyed and Mexico City was built on its ruins. Mexico remained a Spanish colony until the Mexican War of Independence, which began in 1810.*

Glossary

alliance An agreement between two or more groups of people to work together to reach a goal

allies Friends who provide assistance

ancestry The people who one comes from, or is a descendent of

causeway A raised embankment over water that serves as a road

Christianity A religion based on the teachings of Jesus Christ, who Christians believe to be the son of God

class What some people believe to be a person's place in society, usually determined by economic wealth

colonists People who go to a new land to help rule over it and establish settlements

conqueror Someone who takes over using force

conquest The forceful, often violent, takeover of a place or people

empire A group of territories or governments all under the control of one main ruler

governor The official ruler of a place

interpreter A person who translates words from one language into another

intimidate To cause fear

Latin The language of ancient Rome and the Roman Catholic Church

missionaries People who go to another land to try to convert people to their own religion

noble A person of high ranking in society

peasant A poor, landless farmer

priest Someone who performs religious ceremonies

Roman Catholic Church A branch of Christianity. The leader of the Roman Catholic Church is the Pope, in Rome

Index

Printed in the U.S.A.